T0157033

Reflections In A Mirror

Reflections In A Mirror

The Nature Of Appearance In Buddhist Philosophy

Charlie Singer

iUniverse, Inc.
Bloomington

Reflections in a Mirror
The Nature of Appearance in Buddhist Philosophy

Copyright © 2011 by Charlie Singer.

Empty Blue Planet copyright ©1998
The No-Self Nature copyright ©1995
The Last Word in Shalom is OM copyright ©2001

All rights reserved. No part of this book may be used or reproduced by any means, graphic, electronic, or mechanical, including photocopying, recording, taping or by any information storage retrieval system without the written permission of the publisher except in the case of brief quotations embodied in critical articles and reviews.

The views expressed in this work are solely those of the author and do not necessarily reflect the views of the publisher, and the publisher hereby disclaims any responsibility for them.

iUniverse books may be ordered through booksellers or by contacting:

iUniverse
1663 Liberty Drive
Bloomington, IN 47403
www.iuniverse.com
1-800-Authors (1-800-288-4677)

Because of the dynamic nature of the Internet, any web addresses or links contained in this book may have changed since publication and may no longer be valid. The views expressed in this work are solely those of the author and do not necessarily reflect the views of the publisher, and the publisher hereby disclaims any responsibility for them.

Any people depicted in stock imagery provided by Thinkstock are models, and such images are being used for illustrative purposes only.
Certain stock imagery © Thinkstock.

ISBN: 978-1-4620-4656-0 (sc)
ISBN: 978-1-4620-4657-7 (ebk)

Printed in the United States of America

iUniverse rev. date: 08/25/2011

Dedication

To H. H. the Dalai Lama, H.H. Dudjom Rinpoche,
and to all the people of Tibet;

To my parents and to my brother and sister;

And to all the bluesmen and women of the past,
present, and future.

Preface

Reflections in a Mirror was written largely for purposes of the author's own edification, along with the intention of sharing some insights from Tibetan Buddhist tradition with people of various religious or spiritual backgrounds. While not intended as a scholarly presentation, this composition may be of interest to the general reader, who is interested in Buddhist philosophy. For those who wish to follow up their study of some of the topics discussed herein, a recommended reading list is included at the back of the book.

The author gratefully acknowledges the late Ven. Khenchen Palden Sherab for his encouragement, and also for the authorization to include the Vajrayana teachings in this presentation, as well as H. H. Sakya Trizin, Ven. Khenpo Tsewang Dongyal, Ven. Lama Pema Wangdak for kindly providing the Foreword, Ven. Lama Rinchen Puntsok, and all the lamas of the Tibetan Buddhist tradition, for all their kindness and inspiration.

Finally, thanks are extended to Dr. Edwin Bokert, who is an esteemed psychotherapist and a long-time student of Tibetan Buddhism, for providing the introduction; to Marie Blizzard, for typing and preparing the original manuscript; to Dr. Steven Goodman and Jeff Cox for their advice; and to Joy Hansen and everybody at iUniverse; to Dan Menges and Bob Fierman for editorial assistance; and special thanks to Shelley Pearce for sponsoring the production of this book.

Introduction

In the Tibetan medical tradition, the doctors/lamas make small, precious pills that help heal their patients in various ways. Charlie Singer's Reflections in a Mirror is like one of these pills—when you read and digest this small, precious book, it will undoubtedly help.

Like a skilled physician or therapist, the book diagnoses our problems with the "blues" of dissatisfaction, impermanence, and the inevitability of our own demise. The text, again like a good doctor, then prescribes the remedies we need. It discusses how we can begin to heal ourselves by taking refuge in the "three jewels," developing a kind heart, awakening the "mind of enlightenment", and practicing meditation. The treatment is complete with the realization of our non-dual wisdom.

In the western tradition, medical doctors diagnose and treat the patient's body, and psychotherapists treat the client's mind. These approaches are indeed helpful, and yet, without getting at the root cause of all physical illness and mental suffering: ignorance and the attachment to our ego, all other treatments are only temporary and relative. Reflections in a Mirror describes this ultimate healing state, which is none other than our own enlightened nature, the pure, pristine awareness or cognition, which is the true doctor and therapist within us all.

Edwin Bokert,
Ph.D.
March, 2000

Empty Blue Planet

The Primordial Buddha, Samantabhadra, with consort, Samantabhadri

Chapter 1: Blue Planet

From the perspective of a traveler in outer-space, our planet, Earth, may be said to resemble a "big blue marble," floating peacefully in space. If this traveler were a being from another part of the universe, as they approached the surface of the planet, they might be under the impression that they were beholding some sort of paradise, a heavenly realm, where the inhabitants all enjoy lives of complete peace and happiness and well-being.

Here on the surface of the Earth itself, however, this is not the case at all. One need only to pick up the daily newspaper, or watch the evening news, or merely live among other people, to learn of all the many types of problems besetting the inhabitants of our world.

When the historical Buddha, Buddha Shakyamuni, attained enlightenment under the Bodhi tree in Bodhgaya, in India, regarded in Buddhist tradition as being the "central axis of our world system," for some time afterward, he did not teach. Rather, he remained silent, regarding the truth of his realization as being beyond the comprehension of the beings of this world.

Then, encouraged by the gods, Indra and Brahma, he decided to share his message with others, and then first taught about the truth of "duhkha," usually translated as "suffering," as being the fundamental condition of human life and existence.

With the degree of comfort many human beings have attained over the centuries since the time of the Buddha, and with the human realm being a mixture of both pleasant and unpleasant experiences, "suffering" may seem to be rather a harsh translation of the truth to which the Buddha was referring. So perhaps a better explanation of this term found in Sanskrit Buddhist texts would be that, in using the term "duhkha" (or the equivalent term in whichever language the Buddha actually taught), the Buddha meant to say that life can be difficult, or beset with problems, and dissatisfaction.

If the Buddha had first appeared and had taught in America in the twentieth century, perhaps his first teaching might simply be characterized as the truth of "the Blues," as well as the rest of the "four noble truths": the cause of having "the Blues"; the possibility of cessation from having "the Blues"; and the noble (eightfold) path leading to this cessation. So this is another sense in which it can be said that as human beings on the Earth, we inhabit a "blue" planet.

But somewhere between the rather harsh expression of "life is suffering" and the pop-culture expression that "life gives you the Blues," we might say that, based on a careful examination of our lives as human beings, we can agree that the Buddha was correct when he explained in his first teaching that life as a human being (as well as life among the other realms, such as the animal realm) can be unpleasant, and filled with problems and difficulty.

There are various aspects of this "duhkha" explained in the Buddhist teachings. All beings can experience difficulty because of old age, sickness and death. Also there is dissatisfaction, or difficulty, in not having what we would like to have. Having acquired what we wanted to have, it can be unpleasant to worry about losing what we have acquired, and perhaps to struggle to maintain it. Then, it may also be unpleasant when we actually do lose what we once had, what we thought would be a permanent part of our lives.

Because of impermanence and change, at any time, we may lose what we believed was inherently "ours", such as our loved ones and our possessions. What is here one day may be gone the next. Furthermore, sometimes "When it rains it pours" and we may experience what the texts refer to as "suffering on top of suffering," along with this so-called "suffering of change." In addition, we are always subject to what is called the "all pervading suffering of formation," in that, with each passing moment, or each breath we take, we are continually drawing closer to our death.

To determine the cause of this difficulty, or dissatisfaction, inherent in (human) existence, we may look to an explanation of another of the Buddha's fundamental teachings, namely, the doctrine of karma, that is, the principle of cause and effect. According to the Buddha, acting in a virtuous manner will yield a positive result, such as happiness and well-being and positive conditions in this and future lives, while engaging in non-virtuous actions will lead to unfortunate states in future rebirths, and to unhappiness, dissatisfaction, and difficulty in this life. In other words, "Like begets like," or in the words of the Bible, "As you sow, so shall you reap."

Traditionally, ten main types of non-virtuous actions are counted, divided into actions connected to body, speech, and mind, which in Buddhist thought are the three aspects of which a human being is comprised. Three actions are connected to "body," namely: willfully killing another being; stealing, or "taking what is not given"; and sexual misconduct, such as committing adultery.

Four non-virtuous actions are connected to "speech": telling lies; creating divisiveness among others through our speech; speaking harshly to others; and idle chatter. There are also three types of non-virtuous actions in relation to "mind": coveting what others have; wishing harm on other beings; and harboring wrong views about reality. The ten virtuous actions are basically to give up and not indulge in the ten non-virtuous actions.

What we might refer to as "unwholesome" karma can be traced back to what are referred to in Sanskrit Buddhist terminology as the kleshas, that is, the so-called "disturbing emotions." There are many of these kleshas, but in a sense, they can be reduced to five basic emotions: attachment, aversion (or anger), ignorance, pride, and jealousy. It is said in the Buddhist teachings that beings suffer from various difficulties because they continually embody the root of these disturbing emotions.

As for the cause of these mental and emotional disturbances, the source is said to be the ignorance that regards the self and all phenomena to be truly and inherently existent, in a solid, concrete manner. This condition is known as "self-grasping ignorance."

Inwardly, we believe that there is a solid and independent self which is separate from our body and mind, in the manner of an "ego" or an "I" who "inhabits" our body and mind. Outwardly, we accept the belief that all appearances or phenomena in the world around us, partake of the nature of being truly and solidly existing objects, which exist "from their own side," independent of our perception.

According to the Buddha, however, beings and phenomena do not really exist in the solid, independent way that we like to assume or imagine they do. This "no-self' nature of beings and phenomena is known in Sanskrit Buddhist terminology as anatman, and will be discussed in more detail later in this presentation.

In addition, in the Buddha's so-called "first-turning of the wheel of the Dharma" (that is, the Buddhist teachings), along with the teachings on the "four noble truths," he also referred to the "three marks of existence," as the three fundamental conditions underlying human experience. Along with the truths of duhkha and anatman, the Buddha taught that the third underlying principle of existence is impermanence, known in Sanskrit as anitya.

Beings are all subject to death, and objects in our world, such as buildings, are also impermanent. Whatever possessions we possess will eventually be lost at the time of our death—as the saying goes, "You can't take it with you"—and we will all be separated from those we have met during our lifetime. Time is in constant movement, and even friendships and relationships lack true stability.

Perhaps the most prominent aspect of impermanence is death. Whoever is born is certain to die one day, and there is no certainty as to the time, place, or circumstances of our deaths. So these two topics of death and impermanence are best thought of together.

In the Buddhist teachings of the "stages of the path," it is regarded as very important to contemplate these teachings on duhkha (the dissatisfying or difficult aspect of existence, not just of human beings, but all beings in the different realms of existence, such as the animal realm); karma (the principle of cause and effect); and on death and impermanence.

Along with these, there is the contemplation of the precious and valuable circumstance of having had the good fortune to have been born as a human being, and endowed with the opportunity to be able to practice the spiritual path of the Dharma. These four contemplations are sometimes referred to as "the four thoughts that turn the mind." That is, if well contemplated, these "four thoughts" will lead to the individual turning away from an ordinary preoccupation with worldly existence in samsara, the realm of birth, death, and rebirth, which is pervaded by dissatisfaction and impermanence.

Turning the mind to the possibility of traversing the path to the end result of our spiritual evolution, and to the cessation of ordinary samsaric existence, we will direct our intentions to the attainment of the state of enlightenment, and to true peace of mind and well-being. We may be able to follow the noble path of the Buddha and attain for ourselves the same level of complete enlightenment, and become an enlightened being, or a Buddha.

Padmasambhava, the Indian guru who brought the Buddhist teachings to Tibet

Chapter 2: Compassionate Planet

Through contemplating teachings, such as the "four noble truths," and the "four mind-turnings," we gradually develop the conviction that we would like to take advantage of this "precious human rebirth," which is endowed with the freedom to engage in the spiritual practice of the Dharma, and to accomplish what is meaningful. Recognizing the rare opportunity of having been born into the human realm (we need only look around us at all the beings in the animal realm, including the sea creatures and insects, to see that the odds of having a human incarnation are very slight indeed) and regarding samsara as a realm fraught with difficulty and impermanence, we may develop the conviction that we would like to turn our mind away from ordinary worldly preoccupations, and to direct our mind toward the Dharma. In this way, we may be able to accomplish the true purpose of our lives, and to attain complete enlightenment, while we still enjoy the good fortune of having this human body.

Traditionally, the first step in the path of the Dharma, is to take "refuge" or "safe direction" in the so-called "three jewels," namely, in the Buddha, as the supreme teacher; in the Dharma, as the supreme path or teaching; and in the Sangha, that is, the community of those who practice the Dharma. There are different levels of understanding this "refuge" in the "three jewels," but at a deeper level, when we take refuge in the Buddha, for example, we are actually taking refuge in our own ultimate attainment of Buddhahood, or actually in the state of enlightenment itself. According to the supreme Buddhist teachings of Dzogchen (the "Great Perfection"), the highest teachings of the Nyingma school of Tibetan Buddhism, at the ultimate level, we take refuge in the true nature of our mind, or more specifically, in the essence, nature, and capacity of the true nature of mind, a topic which will be discussed later in this book.

Returning to the image of our planet as a "big blue marble floating in space," which may seem from a distance to potentially be some kind of paradise, or perfect realm, we may wonder and ask ourselves, "Where have we gone wrong?"

According to the Buddhist teachings, we experience dissatisfaction and difficulty because of the disturbing emotions (kleshas) which lead to negative karmic actions and their results. As we have seen, these kleshas can be traced back to "self-grasping ignorance," which was discussed earlier. Coupled with this "self-grasping ignorance" is the attitude known as "self-cherishing." That is, we are continually looking out only for our own interests, while neglecting to "cherish others" and to place others ahead of ourselves.

In the Lojong (mind-training) tradition of Tibetan Buddhism, it is said that true happiness can only come from cherishing and benefiting others, and that all unhappiness and difficulty arise from the self-cherishing attitude.

To reverse this condition of the way things have developed in our world because of "self-grasping ignorance" and the self-cherishing attitude, we need to develop a different attitude toward all the beings around us. We can begin to do this with the practice of the so-called "four immeasurables," namely, love, compassion, joy, and equanimity.

First, we can begin to develop an attitude of impartiality, or equanimity, toward all other beings. Usually, we have attachment for our loved ones and friends, and dislike or aversion for those we don't like, or our enemies. In developing equanimity, we don't regard others with an equal sense of indifference or apathy, but treat all beings, without exception, with loving-kindness and compassion.

Through meditating on equanimity, we may come to regard all other beings with love, or loving-kindness. Contemplating that, like ourselves, all beings desire happiness and well-being, and they all do not want unhappiness or problems, we begin to develop love for other beings, which is the wish for others to be happy. Whatever we do, say, or intend in regard to others should be based on a sense of loving-kindness, with others' best interests in mind.

While love is regarded as the wish for other beings to be happy, the emphasis in the attitude of compassion is slightly different, in that here, we develop an attitude of wishing others to be free from any unhappiness or difficulty they may have.

Finally, with the "immeasurable quality" of joy, rather than feeling jealous when other beings are happy or successful, or enjoying anything positive, we rejoice in their good fortune, and wish them continued and increasing well-being and enjoyment.

According to the renowned Tibetan lama of the nineteenth century, Patrul Rinpoche, these four immeasurable qualities can be summarized in the phrase of having "a kind heart."

These four qualities can be regarded as "immeasurable" in the sense that a person can never contemplate and cultivate these qualities too much. The more we work at developing these qualities in ourselves, the deeper will be our realization, and we will be able to embody these qualities in a more direct and authentic manner.

Another source of confusion and difficulty is that of so-called "wrong views." The Buddha claimed that his philosophy embraced "the middle way," avoiding the two extremes of eternalism and nihilism. The eternalist view accepts a truly existent permanent self, contrary to the aforementioned Buddhist teaching of anatman. This view also accepts the existence of an eternally existing creator of the universe. Although many people may be benefited by believing in a creator, or God, there is a sense in which, by believing in a God, we may actually be merely projecting an imagined belief in a truly-existing self onto an imaginary supreme being we regard as also being endowed with a self, and located somewhere in the space above our Earth. In the Buddhist view, there is no self-existing universal consciousness principle existing beyond the consciousness of the individual.

In the nihilist view, along with the belief that "things simply arise by themselves, spontaneously," nihilists deny reincarnation and the idea of past and future lives, as well as karma (cause and effect), and even the possibility of enlightenment and liberation.

In overlooking the truth of reincarnation, a reality recognized by all enlightened beings, who have direct insight into the condition of sentient beings, we lose sight of our relatedness at one time or another, to all other beings to whom we were connected in our previous lives. We have all had countless rebirths since "time immemorial," and according to Buddhist ways of thinking, at one time or another, all other beings have been our mother, or perhaps our father or mother.

Taking this line of thinking a step further, we can then say, that at one time or another, every other being has been our father or mother, or sister or brother, so this may be important to keep in mind in our dealings with others. At the same time, we can regard all our fellow inhabitants of the Earth as being our "brothers and sisters."

After recognizing all beings as having been our parents, we think back and recall all the kindness our parents have shown us in this lifetime. Then we can begin to consider the kindness others must have shown us when we were related to them in past lives. At one time or another, all beings have shown us great kindness.

Reflecting upon the difficult nature of ordinary samsaric existence, and recalling the kindness of all beings, who at one time or another have been a cherished parent or sibling, the natural outcome is to wish to repay their kindness, and to "watch out" for their well-being.

We proceed by developing a sense of affectionate love, which genuinely cherishes other beings, and also a deep sense of compassion, wishing to alleviate the difficulty and unhappiness of all other beings.

Based on this process, beginning with the recognition of all other beings as having at one time or another been one of our parents, we are led to developing the special intention to attain complete enlightenment, the level of a Buddha, so that we will be endowed with the knowledge and capabilities to teach and benefit others, according to their nature and mentality, and to help others attain the true purpose of their existence, the attainment of enlightenment and liberation. The result of this process is the special aspiration to strive to attain enlightenment for the benefit of all sentient beings, and is known as bodhichitta, "the mind of enlightenment."

The first type of bodhichitta is the "relative bodhichitta," and this may be divided into the aspirational or "wishing" bodhichitta, just described, and the "practical" bodhichitta, which traditionally consists of all those activities which accomplish the benefit of all other beings. Those who embody the altruistic intention of the bodhichitta arc known as the Bodhisattvas, and the virtuous activities they practice to benefit others, that is, the practical aspect of the relative bodhichitta, are known as the six (or sometimes, ten) paramitas, or transcendent virtues, sometimes referred to as the six "transcendent perfections."

These six paramitas, consisting of the practices of generosity, morality, patience, joyful effort (consisting of enthusiasm in the performance of virtuous activities), meditation, and transcendent wisdom, correspond to the different levels or stages of the path of the Bodhisattvas, leading to enlightenment, or Buddhahood. As this small book is not intended to be a comprehensive survey of the spiritual path of the Dharma, these six paramitas should be studied about in greater depth elsewhere, such as in the classic text, the Bodhicaryavatara (A Guide to the Bodhisattva's Way of Life), by the Indian Buddhist teacher, Shantideva, who is said to have been a previous incarnation of the aforementioned nineteenth century Tibetan lama, Patrul Rinpoche.

Traditionally, the combined formula for taking "refuge" in the "three jewels," and generating the aspiration for enlightenment, the bodhichitta, (or the Bodhisattva vow), is expressed as follows:

"In the Buddha, Dharma, and Sangha, I take refuge until enlightenment is attained. Through the merit of generosity and the other perfections, May I attain Buddhahood for the sake of all beings."

Buddha Shakyamuni

Chapter 3: Empty Planet

The ultimate aspect of the bodhichitta, or "the mind of enlightenment," involves developing the correct view, which in the context of Mahayana and Vajrayana Buddhism, is the realization of emptiness, known in Sanskrit as "shunyata."

Earlier, we spoke of the self-grasping ignorance (atmagraha-avidya), as the source of the disturbing-emotions, and the dissatisfaction and difficulty to which they lead. As we said, inwardly we accept the belief in a truly-existing self, or "I" which we imagine to exist independently of our body and mind, and outwardly, we believe that all phenomena, or objects, have true inherent existence, independent of our perception, as if they exist independently "from their own side."

At the level of the "first-turning of the wheel of Dharma," the level of the so-called Hinayana teachings, the Buddha spoke in terms of beings and phenomena as partaking of the nature of selflessness, or no-self (anatman). The term used at the level of the second and third turnings of "the wheel of Dharma" by the Buddha, the level of the Mahayana teachings, is that persons (and all beings) and phenomena (objects and appearances) are "empty" or "shunya" (tong-pa in Tibetan); that their nature is the great emptiness or "shunyata" (or tong-pa-nyid in Tibetan). In a sense, although the terminology used is different, the meaning of the reality to which these terms, anatman and shunyata, refer, is essentially not different.

Traditionally, first we examine the nature of the individual, or person. If we investigate our embodiment, we can "search" the inside of our body, trying to determine where, or in which part of our body, the self or "I" is located, or exists. Mentally "dissecting" our body, composed of flesh, blood, bones, internal organs, sense organs, muscle, tissue, and so forth, we can try to determine where it is that the self we imagine to inhabit our body, is located.

Some people may imagine that their self, or "I", is located in the region of the heart, while the common tendency among most people is to imagine that the self, the one we refer to commonly as "me," is located in the head, and gazes out at the outside world from this stable vantage point "behind our eyes." Searching inwardly carefully, however, we may come to realize that there is no self located somewhere in our body; that this imagined self is "empty" of inherent existence, or "empty" of true and independent existence.

However, dependent upon factors, such as body, mind, and name, we may accept, or designate, a conventionally-existing self or "I." On the basis of a person having a conventionally-accepted existence, we can accept statements, such as, "There are three people in the room," to be relatively valid, and on this basis we can, for example, practice virtuous actions, such as abstaining from killing, or harming others. But at the level of ultimate truth, this self or "I" is found to be "empty" of true existence, as "the one who inhabits our body and mind (and has a name)."

In regard to the mind, we can examine the belief that there is a self or "I" who exists as "the one who inhabits our mind" and has thoughts (or thinks). In common sense thinking, it seems perfectly normal to "talk to ourselves all day," that is, to have "mental conversations with oneself," believing that there is a self or an "I" (the individual we refer to as "me", or refer to by our name), who is saying and hearing the thoughts "in our head."

This state of affairs must also be investigated. Through study, reflection, and meditation on the "empty" nature of the person, we may be able to penetrate to the true condition of what is actually involved in the situation we normally call "a person thinking" or having thoughts.

We may attend to the observation of the state of stillness (that is, being without thought), and look with awareness to see if there is a self, who is "not having thoughts." When thoughts occur, we can look to see if there is actually an individual, or "I", who is having the thoughts. Looking with awareness, we may come to realize that the awareness does not have a self "behind it," but arises without self-nature.

The nature of mind is such that the mind is "empty of self nature," (or of having a self who "inhabits" the mind). Yet, it is still endowed with a cognizant, or knowing quality, and as a natural expression of the mind, thoughts arise as the creative expression, or display, of the mind. If we mistakenly believe that these thoughts "belong to" our self, that there is an independent "I" who is thinking these thoughts, we go astray and are caught up in the state of dualistic-ignorance, known as avidya, in Sanskrit, or ma-rig-pa, in Tibetan.

On the other hand, it is possible to recognize that the self is ultimately non-existent, and that our thoughts are not so solid, and do not "belong to" a self or "I." Instead, these thoughts may be recognized as being merely the "creative play" or natural expression, of the true nature of mind, and devoid of self-nature. Rather than being caught up in dualistic-ignorance and the workings of the ordinary mind, known as sem in Tibetan, we will be beyond any subject/object duality and our mind may be characterized as non-dualistic awareness, called rigpa in Tibetan (vidya being the Sanskrit equivalent).

This non-dual awareness, or intrinsic awareness, of rigpa, also includes awareness of the true nature of appearances, or phenomena. After developing direct insight into the empty nature of the person, or self, we can direct our attention to the way in which the objects of the five senses (seeing, hearing, smelling, tasting, and touching) are also devoid of a truly-existing self nature.

One approach is to become more aware of the process by which we impute true existence to an object, through what we might call "mental labeling." For example, we may search for the bases of such designations as "cat" or "bird" or any other so-called thing. Although the eyes, nose, flesh, blood, bones, and so forth, each have their own name, no bases for the designations "cat" or "bird" can be found to exist objectively.

Similarly, among inanimate objects, the term "chair" is not used for the wood, the legs, the seat, or the back of the chair; in none of the component parts can an object designated as "chair" be found to objectively exist. Other things are alike in only existing at a conventional level through being designated as such through "mental labeling."

In a different manner of approach, we look into the "empty" nature of appearances or objects in terms of developing awareness of the sense in which phenomena exist, not in an independent way "outside of us," but as completely inseparable from the inherent nature of our mind, and our perception of these so-called "things." In this approach, we look to the inseparability of appearance and mind.

For example, suppose we are looking at a house across the street. In ordinary dualistic thinking, we think that there is a truly existing object "over there," which exists independently of our perception. We believe there is a definite boundary, or separation, between our body "here" and the object we see "there." We think that we will walk across the distance to this house we regard as being "a thing taking up space in a place," and which truly exists "out there." Taking this line of reasoning further, we consider that we will go inside this house, and once inside, we will be looking at other truly-existing objects, such as walls, floors, ceilings, and objects, such as tables, chairs, and "knick-knacks."

Ultimately, this house, the tables, chairs, and so on, are alike in being a mere appearance within the realm of our non-dual intrinsic awareness, or rigpa. These so-called objects are inseparable from our mind, (similar in nature to a mirror and its reflections), and in the same manner of thoughts being a natural expression of the nature of mind, appearances, too, arise as the natural, creative display of our intrinsic awareness, (or, rigpa'i-tsal in Tibetan).

On the one hand, we have a mind, which is empty in essence, and yet is cognizant (or "luminous") in nature, with a knowing capacity which is able to reflect apparent phenomena with complete clarity. In regard to phenomena, these appearances are said to appear while ultimately being not truly-existent. As to their essence, phenomena are "empty" of being truly existent; while in regard to their nature, they are manifest and appear. The inseparability of these two aspects is known as "capacity."

This nature of reality is expressed in the language of the Heart Sutra (the most well-known of the Prajnaparamita Sutras of the Buddha) as "Form is empty; emptiness is form." In the tradition of Mahamudra, this is known as the inseparability of appearance and emptiness (nangtong-yermed); while the Lamdre, or "Path and the

Fruit" tradition of the Sakya school of Tibetan Buddhism, regards the supreme view as "the inseparability of luminosity (or clarity) and emptiness," (saltong-yermed). The Dzogchen tradition of Tibetan Buddhism refers to the empty aspect of mind and phenomena as "primordial purity" (kadag in Tibetan), and the luminous, or cognizant aspect, (that is, while things are "empty," still perceptions occur) as "spontaneous presence" (lhundrub in Tibetan.).

There are different types of the aforementioned Mahamudra: Sutra Mahamudra; Tantric Mahamudra; and Essence Mahamudra. Traditionally, it is said that Essence Mahamudra and the Dzogchen view of "the cutting-through of primordial purity," (known as kadag-trekcho in Tibetan), are alike in explaining the nature of mind and reality as being characterized by the inseparable union of intrinsic awareness (rigpa) and "emptiness" (or, rigtong-yermed in Tibetan).

The white form of Vajrasattva

Chapter 4: Empty Blue Planet

In the supreme Buddhist teaching, known as Dzogchen (or, the "Great Perfection"), a student with the suitable karma to be endowed with great intelligence, and having devotion to a qualified teacher, who is an authentic "holder of awareness," (or, vidyadhara in Sanskrit) of these teachings, can be directly introduced to the rigpa nature of mind, and receive the direct transmission, pointing out the recognition of the true nature of mind and reality.

Traditionally, it is necessary to have first gone through different stages, or preliminaries and then, when the conditions are right, the teacher (or lama, in Tibetan) will introduce the disciple to the non-dual intrinsic awareness of rigpa. This rigpa is inseparable from the pristine awareness (called yeshe in Tibetan) of the Dharmakaya, the mind which directly perceives the ultimate, empty nature of (persons and) phenomena.

In the Dzogchen teachings, the Dharmakaya (the so-called "body of truth" of a Buddha) is personified as the naked blue primordial Buddha, Samantabhadra (the "All-Good"), sometimes depicted in union with the while female consort, Samantabhadri. "The mind of Samantabhadra" is synonymous with rigpa, and whereas ordinary sentient beings wander from lifetime to lifetime in confusion because of being unaware of their true nature, Samantabhadra is aware of "his" enlightened nature.

When the student is directly introduced to the pristine awareness (yeshe) of the Dharmakaya, he/she is said to "recover the mind of Samantabhadra," or his/her own intrinsic awareness of rigpa; i.e., the awareness of the Buddha-nature, or the nature of mind, and the true nature of reality (dharmata in Sanskrit).

The meditation of Dzogchen consists simply of remaining in the view of the pristine awareness of the Dharmakaya to which the student has been directly introduced.

Traditionally, this meditation consists of the wisdom which recognizes the true nature (of mind and reality), inseparable from loving-kindness and compassion. This compassion arises naturally toward all beings, who experience difficulty or unhappiness through not being aware of their true nature.

The action or conduct of Dzogchen is to never be separated from the view, and the result or fruition is said to be simply to allow the view to go on in an uninterrupted manner.

In the well-known "three-fold testament" (known as the Tsigsum-Nedeg in Tibetan) of the first human Dzogchen master, Garab Dorje, the first "statement" is the "direct introduction to rigpa." This rigpa-nature has been explained in Chapter 3.

Having been introduced by the teacher to our Buddha nature (known in Sanskrit as the sugatagarbha) as the non-dual awareness of rigpa, embodying the empty-luminous nature of mind, the second statement, then, is to "decide on one point."

Recognizing that all phenomena of samsara and nirvana (or liberation) are the creative display, or the dynamic energy (tsal) of the state of intrinsic awareness, or rigpa, we come to a definitive decision about the state of knowledge, and know that there is nothing which is not included in the state of rigpa, and we should continue in this state of awareness.

In being introduced to our true Buddha-nature as the awareness of the empty essence of mind, luminous or cognizant nature, and their inseparable union, we recognize the empty essence as the Dharmakaya; the luminous. nature as the Sambhogakaya (the "body of enjoyment" of a Buddha); and the unity of the empty essence and the luminous nature, as the Nirmanakaya ("emanation-body") of a Buddha.

Thus, as the second of Garab Dorje's "three statements," we can come to the conclusion that the state of enlightenment, the attainment of the three "bodies" (or, kayas in Sanskrit) of a Buddha, is not somewhere outside us, to be attained elsewhere, but is already inherent in our own true nature of mind, or as it is expressed traditionally, "in the palm of our hand."

The third statement is known as, "gaining confidence in liberation." Here, we are continually aware of the empty nature of thoughts and emotions, and the manner in which they arise from our mind and dissolve back into our mind, similar to the way in which waves arise from and dissolve back into the ocean. Whereas, in ordinary dualistic mind (sem), we regard thoughts and emotions as belonging to a self or "I" who is, as it were, like an "owner" of the thoughts and emotions, and who reacts to them with different feelings of like and dislike, acceptance and rejection, in the process of "self-liberation," thoughts and emotions are recognized directly as the natural display, or the creative energy of intrinsic awareness, and arise from and dissolve back into the empty awareness of the Dharmakaya.

According to the great Dzogchen master, Vimalamitra, there are three levels of this practice of self-liberation, and at the most advanced level, thoughts, as well as emotions, are likened to "a thief in an empty house." That is, having no self "behind them," there is no reason to be disturbed, or elated by these thoughts and emotions, and there is no benefit or harm to be derived, just like a thief in an empty house, who finds nothing to steal and can cause no harm or disturbance, or receive any benefit for himself. In other words, ultimately, thoughts and emotions are neither helpful nor harmful.

Having mentioned the topic of the emotions, at this point, it may be helpful to look more closely at the nature of these ("disturbing") emotions.

Through "self-grasping ignorance," inwardly, we conceive of a self or "I" as a truly-existing agent, who seems to inhabit our body and mind; and outwardly, we conceive of phenomena and appearances as being truly-existent objects "out-there," and inherently separate from us, rather than recognizing their condition as being a mere "ornament" of our non-dual awareness of rigpa, or merely an apparitional-like presentation from which we are ultimately not separate. It is said that, from the confusion of the thought of "I" arises the thought "mine," and then we proceed to grasp at so-called "things," to confirm, or solidify our existence.

With the dualistic concepts of self and phenomena as independent and truly-existing entities, the emotions arise as the "glue that holds the whole picture together." It is for this reason that in the Buddhist visual teaching image called "the wheel of life," at the center, or hub, of the wheel of samsara, are the rooster, snake, and pig, which symbolize the emotions of attachment (or desire), aversion (or anger), and ignorance, respectively. Along with these three emotions that "turn the wheel of life," are usually counted the other two basic emotions with which an imagined self can relate to phenomena (including the phenomena of "other beings"), namely, pride and jealousy.

At the different levels of the Buddhist teachings, the emotions are dealt with in different ways. We have already discussed the self-liberation of thoughts and emotions, according to the Dzogchen teachings.

At the level of the Hinayana, it is regarded as advisable to completely renounce, or abandon, the emotions as something completely undesirable. At the level of the Mahayana Buddhist practice, it is recommended to apply the appropriate "antidote," meditating, for example, on love as the antidote to anger or aversion.

At the level of the approach of Vajrayana, or Tantric Buddhism, the practitioner regards the five emotions (attachment, aversion, ignorance, pride, and jealousy) in the form of symbolic Tantric archetype-deities, which embody the transformed aspect of these emotions. These are known in Vajrayana Buddhism (the Buddhism of Tibet, which also contains the other two levels of Hinayana and Mahayana), as the five pristine "wisdoms," or the five pristine awarenesses.

If we recognize the empty nature of desire, or attachment, rather than grasping after a so-called truly-existing object we have singled out as something we desire and long to have, we understand or recognize the empty nature of this apparitional-like object, which has been singled out from the field of our awareness. This emotion of attachment is transformed into the pristine awareness, or wisdom (yeshe) known as the "wisdom of discrimination," represented by the symbolic archetype-deity, called Buddha Amitabha, depicted with a red body, the color of passion or desire. When Amitabha is depicted in union with a female consort, the nature of this consort is related to the corresponding element of fire.

Like attachment, ignorance, the emotion in which we do not see things clearly as they really are, is said to pervade the other four emotions. The transformed aspect of ignorance, is characterized by a direct, non-conceptual understanding of emptiness. This "wisdom of the Dharmadhatu" (the empty realm of phenomena) is symbolized by the white Buddha, known in Sanskrit as Vairochana. His symbolic consort is related to the element of water.

Similarly, pride, or feeling superior to others, is transformed into the "wisdom of equality," or the "equalizing wisdom," which is beyond dualistic conceptions of good or bad, superior or inferior, and so forth, and is pervaded by a sense of perfect equanimity, and a sense of all other beings as ultimately having the same true nature as ourselves. This "wisdom" is embodied by the symbolic yellow Buddha, Ratnasambhava, whose consort is also yellow in color, and embodies the element of earth.

The "all-accomplishing wisdom" represents the transformed aspect of jealousy, and rather than feeling jealous about what someone else has accomplished, with this pristine awareness, appropriate actions are spontaneously accomplished to benefit others. This pristine "wisdom" is symbolized by the Buddha Amogasiddhi, who is green, the color of envy or jealousy in the Tantric system, and depicted in union with a green female consort who embodies the element of air.

Finally, anger, or aversion, which is directed at apparent objects we regard as undesirable (including certain other people), is purified, or transformed into the "mirror-like wisdom," which merely reflects the apparitional object clearly, like an image appearing in the "magic-mirror" of our mind. This "wisdom" is embodied by the blue Buddha Akshobhya, or by Vajrasattva, (who can appear as white or blue), and whose consort embodies the element, space.

These "five wisdoms," or pristine awarenesses, are regarded to be an inherent aspect of our Buddha-nature, along with the three kayas of a Buddha: the Dharmakaya (our empty essence); the Sambhogakaya (our luminous or cognizant nature); and the Nirmanakaya (as the union of the other two kayas), whose "energy" is characterized as "all-pervasive compassion."

When we recognize the Dzogchen view of our true nature, as an embodiment of non-dual intrinsic awareness, simply by training in and continually sustaining that awareness; and finally, completely stabilizing that awareness, we actualize the result or fruition of the spiritual path, attaining the level of a completely enlightened being, or a Buddha, endowed with the four kayas: the above-mentioned three kayas (or trikaya, in Sanskrit), plus the Svabhavikakaya, as the inseparable union of the other three kayas; and the five pristine awarenesses, or "primordial wisdoms" of a Buddha. These four kayas and five "wisdoms" are the inherent qualities of the Buddha-nature, which exist as a potential to be actualized by all beings, and primordially are already our inherent nature.

To re-summarize, when, through the process of recognizing, training in, and completely stabilizing our awareness of our Buddha-nature (sugatagarbha), we "recover the mind of Samantabhadra," and actualize our potential, as beings who, since beginningless time, have been endowed with the ultimate nature of being a Buddha.

It is interesting to note that the term for Buddha, in Tibet, is not Buddha, but sang-gye. The term sang refers to the purification of all our negative characteristics, and of our emotional and conceptual obscurations (that is, any factors which cover over our true nature); and gye refers to the developing or perfecting of the potential of all our positive qualities.

As human beings, we embody the potential to purify any negative aspects of our nature, and to completely perfect, or develop, all our positive qualities, so that we can actualize our complete potential for enlightenment as embodied beings. At the same time, as all beings inherently possess the Buddha-nature, we have, at an ultimate level, embodied the enlightened qualities of all the kayas and "wisdoms," "since time immemorial."

We can try to recognize all the inhabitants of our planet, as the embodiment of all the positive, potential qualities, such as wisdom, kindness, and compassionate activity; and at the same time, be aware that all beings already inherently exist at the present time, as divine-like embodiments, or as "Buddhas in a pure realm"

Whereas, in religious traditions, such as the Judeo Christian tradition, the human beings and their God, or deity, are related to each other, somewhat in the manner of a devoted servant and a master, (similar to the level of Tantric Buddhism known as kriya-yoga tantra), at the higher levels of Vajrayana (or Tantric) Buddhism, we recognize ourselves as having the deity nature ourselves.

This deity-nature is not in the manner of a truly-existing ego, or self who regards him/herself as a God. Rather, from the state of the awareness of emptiness, the luminous aspect appears as oneself in the form of a deity.

For example, according to the text called the Kun Byed Gyalpo ("The Sovereign All-Creating King"), the main text from the section of the Dzogchen teachings, known as the Mind-section, or Semde, the level of the Dzogchen teachings that is said to correspond to the aforementioned Mahamudra (the "Great Seal") teachings, as a practice of guru-yoga (a practice to attain union with the spiritual teacher), we visualize ourselves as the blue Vajrasattva, with a small figure of (the Dharmakaya Buddha) Samantabhadra visualized just above our head. Both Vajrasattva and Samantabhadra are blue in this practice, and may be visualized without a female consort, or with Vajrasattva's consort being light blue here, and Samantabhadra's consort, Samantabhadri (also known as "the Great Mother") being white.

Vajrasattva embodies all Buddhas and all five pristine awarenesses, or "wisdoms," and in this practice, Samantabhadra represents the principle of the spiritual teacher (or guru, in Sanskrit). To develop the proper motivation, first we can recite three times (verbally or mentally) the combined refuge and bodhichitta (the Bodhisattva vow) formula.

Then we can practice the so-called "vajra (or, diamond) recitation," using the sacred mantra-syllables, OM AH HUM, (the vowel sound in HUM sounding like the vowel sound in the word, "good"). These three syllables embody the "energy," respectively, of the enlightened Body, Speech, and Mind. With every inhalation, we think, or mentally recite, OM; at the moment of the brief pause after inhaling, we mentally recite, AH; and while exhaling, we mentally recite, HUM. We do this for as long as we like, combining OM AH HUM with respectively, inhalation, the pause after inhaling, and exhalation.

These three mantra-syllables are regarded in "Tantric science" as being the actual vibrational sounds that accompany the three phases of the breathing process. Through this practice of "vajra-repetition," we can "tune-into," or attain union with, the enlightened nature of Body, Speech, and Mind. Also, repetition of these three syllables is said to purify all negative conditions, including sicknesses, and to prolong our life.

Sometimes, we can recite the six-syllable purification mantra of Vajrasattva: Om Vajrasattva Hum. This mantra purifies all negative actions, habitual tendencies, and both emotional and conceptual obscurations.

At other times, we can also recite the mantra of the primordial Buddha, or Adi-Buddha, Samantabhadra: Om Samantabhadra Ah.

If we are so inclined, we can sometimes recite (verbally or mentally) the hundred syllable mantra of Vajrasattva. This sacred mantra contains the essence of the 100 Peaceful and Wrathful Buddhas (or archetype-deities) which appear to the consciousness of the deceased in the intermediate state (called bardo in Tibetan) after death. This one hundred syllable mantra is regarded to be the supreme mantra for purification, although in general, the six-syllable mantra of Vajrasattva may be regarded as containing the same essence.

Om Benzar Sato Samaya, Manu Palaya

Benzar Sato Tei No Pa, Tisthira Dridho Me Bawa

Suto Khayo Mei Ba WaSu Po Khayo Mei Ba Wa, , Anu Rakto Me Ba Wa

Sar Wa Siddhi Mei Pra Yatsa, Sarwa Karma Sutsa Me,

Tsi Tam Shri Yam Kuru Hung, Ha Ha Ha Ha Ho Bagawan

Sarwa Tathagata, Benzar Ma Mei Muntsa

Benzi Bhawa Maha Samaya Sato Ah

In addition, we might add that, traditionally, in the practice-oriented lineages of Tibet, the two most important attributes accompanying the practice of the spiritual path, are said to be devotion to the teacher, and to all enlightened beings, and compassion for all beings.

In this regard, along with the repetition of mantras during meditation, (these mantras can also be practiced at any suitable time if they do not interfere with one's activities, if so desired), we can also perform the esoteric activity known as "emanating and reabsorbing" in order to benefit all beings "secretly."

We can visualize a small blue Tibetan syllable, HUM (above) in the center of our heart region, with the syllable standing on a white lunar disc, which in turn rests on the eight-petalled lotus of our heart-center. Around this standing blue syllable, is the six or 100 syllable mantra of Vajrasattva.

From these syllables, first we imagine, or visualize, five colored light (red, white, blue, yellow, and green), or if we prefer, clear white light containing the essence of these five colors, emanating, or going out, from our heart center and "going up" to the objects of devotion, that is, to all the enlightened beings (or Buddhas) in the so-called "ten-directions." Pleased with this symbolic "offering," the enlightened beings "send back" the (five colored) light, which dissolves back into the mantra in our heart, and the blue Tibetan syllable, HUM, and we imagine that we receive the blessings of all the Buddhas.

Then, we focus on the object of our compassion, that is, all sentient beings, and we imagine, or visualize, that the light again goes out, this time to all beings, and dissolves into their hearts (and all of their body/minds), and we then imagine that they are all perfectly benefited, according to their individual needs. This practice can enable a person to accumulate a great deal of merit and wisdom, which, according to tradition, are both needed to attain enlightenment, and also benefits all beings everywhere.

At the end of the meditation session, we imagine the small blue figure of Samantabhadra dissolving into light, which enters through the crown of our head, and dissolves into the region of our heart, (the seat of the mind in Vajrayana Buddhist philosophy). We can then rest in the "natural state of mind," remaining in the awareness of the sugatagarbha (the Buddha nature), consisting of the inseparable unity of emptiness, luminosity (or cognizance), and compassion.

Practicing the "self-liberation" of thoughts as they arise, we engage in the profound practice of the "cutting-through" (trekcho) of solidity. That is, relaxing more and more in the rigpa nature, we "cut through" the solidity of the ego, and the thoughts and emotions, continually "self-liberating" all appearances, thoughts, and emotions, as they arise within our awareness.

At the close of the session, we can "dedicate the merit" from our meditation to all other beings and add prayers or aspirations for all beings to realize their true nature, and to attain enlightenment, (as well as any additional aspirations), and then gently arise from the meditation session, while maintaining ongoing awareness, or mindfulness.

In this system of practice, we can also regard all other beings as Vajrasattva, regarding all males as the blue (or white) Vajrasattva, and all females as the light-blue (or white) female counterpart, known in Tibetan as Nyema. We can regard all places as the sacred pure-realm of Vajrasattva, all sounds as mantra, and all thoughts as the "play" of wisdom-awareness. Finally, we can view all appearances as being like a dream or an apparition in nature.

Of course, anyone sincerely interested in practicing the Buddhist teachings, should find a qualified teacher with whom they have a karmic connection, and this is especially true for the Vajrayana teachings. What we have been discussing has been mentioned largely in the interest of sharing some of the insights and aspects of Tibetan Buddhist tradition, as well as for purposes of the author's own edification.

To conclude, we might say that there is a sense in which our realm we call the Earth is already an inherently pure, and sacred realm, just like a traveler from another region of the universe, visiting for the first time, might imagine it to be, before he/she actually landed on the surface of the planet, and then became aware of all the confusion, aggression, and difficulties and problems, that beset human (and other) beings at this time around the beginning of the third millennium of our era.

Through reflecting upon the Buddhist principles we have been discussing regarding the nature of (human) existence, it is evident that, through study, reflection, and meditation on the principles of the Dharma, such as the importance of compassion, and the wisdom aspect of the nature of mind and reality, it may definitely be possible to transform ourselves and our world.

By sharing our wisdom, and benefiting others with the appropriate actions, or skillful means, we can all, both the inhabitants of the planet, and our realm we refer to in the English language as "the Earth," actualize and attain our true and inherent potential.

Recognizing that the true nature of mind is the source of everything, we can realize that it is through the transformation of our minds and our attitudes that true and lasting peace and happiness will come about for all beings, as together, we all develop our potential for enlightened existence.

Author's Colophon: The text of Empty Blue Planet was composed during the auspicious first month of the Earth-Tiger year (1998). Through this merit, may all beings be benefited.

Afterword

If this empty-blue-planet were a musician, it would undoubtedly be a blues musician, and would probably express its understanding of the Mind, as being the primary source of all problems or difficulty, or of "the Blues" (the first and second "noble truths" of the Buddha, traditionally known as "suffering and the cause of suffering").

At the same time, this blue Earth might look forward to a time when, through practicing the spiritual path (the fourth "noble truth," known as "the path"), all the inhabitants of this realm of the Earth, would attain the cessation (the third "noble truth" of the Buddha), of problems, dissatisfaction, and difficulty—the so-called "Blues." Or, in the words of a well-known traditional Blues song:

Trouble in Mind, I'm blue,
But I won't be blue always
The sun's gonna shine,
In my back door someday.

The No-Self Nature

Nagarjuna, Founder of the Madhyamaka Philisophy

Foreword

The wisdom of prajnaparamita is acquired not instantly, but gradually. Sakya Pandita, Kunga Gyaltsen Pal Zangpo's trilogy of study, reflection, and meditation as the approach toward the realization of this profound wisdom is reflected in the author's intent in writing ***The No-Self Nature***. The absolute wisdom is subject to the individual's own realization, and the text of this composition is one of the ways for those who seek the absolute wisdom of the prajnaparamita. I rejoice in his sincere effort in interpreting the Wisdom. This certainly is in the tradition of the "wise ones."

As long as the ocean of the Tathagata's teachings remains on this earth, may this drop of Dharma contribution benefit others as well.

Lama Pema Wangdak
July 30th, 1994

Buddha Shakyamuni

In the history of ideas, there is perhaps no idea more unusual than the Buddhist concept of anatman, or "no-self" This idea of anatman or "no-self" was taught by the historical Buddha, Buddha Shakyamuni, as being one of the "three marks of existence", along with duhkha, or dissatisfaction, and anitya, or impermanence. These three "marks of existence" are regarded in Buddhist thought as being the three fundamental characteristics which pervade the human condition. The three "marks of existence" of dissatisfaction, impermanence and "no-self" have been much written about in the Buddhist literature now available in the English language, but the doctrine of anatman, or "no-self" can be especially difficult to penetrate and represents one of the most unusual, and yet important, ideas to arise in the history of ideas.

Common to all schools, or forms, of Buddhism, is the idea of the anatman, or "no-self" nature of the individual or person (or actually of all beings endowed with consciousness). The Buddha was born into the Hindu religious culture and one of the fundamental tenets of the Hindu religion has always been that all beings are endowed with the nature of (having an) atman, or "soul" or actually a "self", which is ultimately identical with, or actually partakes of, the nature of Brahman, or the creator aspect of God in Hindu tradition. The Buddha never explicitly affirmed or denied the existence of a God, encouraging his disciples to study and practice his teachings until they themselves had attained the level of a perfectly enlightened being, or a Buddha, at which point they would have a direct understanding of this and other such metaphysical questions. However, the Buddha made it quite clear in one of his first teachings, that in regard to the notion that beings are endowed with an atman or permanent "self", that this notion is ultimately erroneous, and that, in fact, the condition of having "no-self" is an underlying "fact-of-life", or principle of existence.

This idea of there being "no-self" can be analyzed in different ways, but from one point of view, we might say that the idea of "no-self" means that when we investigate the nature of the individual or person, if we investigate what is involved carefully enough, we would find that ultimately there isn't actually a "self", or the one we refer to as "I" or "me", as a truly existing being who "inhabits" our body and mind, in a concrete, ongoing, and permanent way. In common sense thinking, and even in traditional philosophies and religious and scientific thinking, there is a sense in which people have always accepted the belief that there is, in fact, a "self" who inhabits our body and mind, who is the one we refer to as "I" or "me."

This attitude, or underlying presupposition of existence, can well be summed up by the statement of the French philosopher, Descartes, that "I think, therefore I am." From the point of view of Buddhist philosophy, however, this sort of statement partakes of the nature of delusion. We might assume that there is a "self" who inhabits our body and mind and is "the one who does our thinking", but if we were to investigate this state of affairs, we would find, according to Buddhist philosophy, that this is, in fact, not the case. Our thoughts and thinking processes might seem as if there is an actual "I" who is generating or thinking our thoughts, saying and hearing the thoughts that arise in our "minds", but if we were to investigate what is actually involved, we might find that, in fact, this notion of an ongoing "self" or "I" is only an erroneous assumption. This idea of there being a "self" is so deep-seated that it may seem completely unquestionable and a "given" factor of experience and existence, but ultimately, according to Buddhist philosophy, the belief in a "self" as being "truly-existing" is a false view.

We might say that thoughts arise as if they "belong to" or are being thought by an ongoing individual, or "self" or "I", but ultimately there is a sense in which "there may not be anybody there!" What is involved might be said to be like a case of "the talk in our heads" pretending to be a "somebody who is having thoughts." Although the common sense belief may be that "I am the one who creates the thoughts", it may be, in fact, that our thinking or thoughts actually help to create the belief that there is a "self" or an "I" who truly exists as "the one who does our thinking!"

Although it is possible to "unravel" what is involved in regard to the nature of the "thinker" and the "thoughts" through practicing different kinds of Buddhist meditation, such as meditation in which we attend to the nature of our thoughts and how they arise in our mind, developing tranquility and direct insight into what is actually involved, it will not be the purpose of this book to discuss the subject of formal meditation, as this is a complicated subject, and because formal meditation is best learned from a qualified meditation teacher.

Instead, we will focus next on the notion of "no-self" as it relates to our sense-perceptions. It is said in Buddhist tradition that the sense of hearing is the easiest of our sense-perceptions by which we can come to an understanding of the nature of "no-self" and, in fact, it is said that the Bodhisattva Avalokiteshvara the personification of the compassion of all the Buddhas, (the reader is reminded that in Buddhist tradition, anyone who has attained the level of a completely enlightened being, or Buddha, is designated as being a Buddha; thus, there have actually been many Buddhas) attained enlightenment by following the advice of Manjushri, the personification of the wisdom of all the Buddhas, and attending to the true nature of the sensation of hearing or sound. If we consider the nature of an ongoing sound, such as a waterfall or even any sounds, such as music, we can ask ourselves "which part of this sound, or auditory presentation, is 'the actual sound' and which part is the 'self' or 'I' who is 'the one who is doing the hearing'?" More specifically, where do we "cut-up" this auditory sensation into the separate components of "the one who hears" and "that which is being heard"? It may be, as with our act of thinking, that we have wrongly assumed the idea of a solid, permanent "self" who acts as an agent or subject, interacting with our sense-perceptions, here being our perception of sound. That is, we regard "ourselves" as being separate subjects which interact with sensations we regard as being truly existing and separate from "us" in a way that the sensations are regarded as separate and independent objects.

As the reader may have noticed, it is very difficult to speak of the non-existent nature of a "self" without discussing the nature of our world of "things" and sensations. Although the idea of the ultimate non-existence of the "self" is a central idea in all forms of Buddhism, of the divisions of Hinayana, Mahayana and Vajrayana Buddhism, in the latter two forms of Buddhism, along with the idea of the ultimate non-existence of the "self", there is also the idea that what we regard as being the world of "things" and sensations, also partakes of the nature of "anatman" or "no-self."

As we have seen in the analysis of sound, such as a waterfall or music, it is very difficult to separate the sensation into a separate subject who is having or experiencing the sensation, and a separate object, that is "the sound being heard." In the Buddhist literature of Abhidharma, rather than accepting the common sense notion that there is a "self" who is a concrete, permanent, truly existing agent which acts as the subject of our sensations, such as seeing and hearing, sensations were analyzed or "broken down" into their apparent component parts. For example, rather than saying that "I see a thing", in the Abhidharma analysis, it would be stated that in the act of visual sensation, it is necessary to have three separate components: a visual sense organ, visual consciousness, and an object of sight.

Whether we analyze "things" and sensations as being sensed or perceived by a central "self" who perceives all the various sensations of the different senses, or analyze them according to the Abhidharma view, according to the view of the philosophical school of the Madhyamaka, a Mahayana Buddhist school founded by the second-century philosopher, Nagarjuna, which was based upon the Prajnaparamita Sutras of the Buddha, the "things" and sensations in our world also partake of the nature of "anatman" or "no-self" in the same way that persons or individuals partake of the "no-self" nature.

As we have said, the nature of the hearing sensation may be the easiest means by which to understand the relationship between a perceiving subject and the object of perception, or actually, to recognize that they are both equally non-existent, ultimately. Rather than being the case that a subject (or a specific variety of sense consciousness, according to the Abhidharma) interacts with and senses (or "grasps" as it is said in the Buddhist philosophical literature) an object of perception, it may be that sensations arise in a way that there is ultimately no subjective pole of experience interacting with a separate objective pole. Because sensations arise beyond the realm of an independent or separate subjective pole, and an independent or separate objective pole, and thus, without any interaction between a subjective and an objective pole or dimension, all our sensations, according to the view of Madhyamaka philosophy, partake of the anatman or "no-self" nature. The technical term, used in the Madhyamaka literature, is that all our sensations, visual, audial, and all others are "shunya" or "empty" or that they partake of the nature of "shunyata" or "emptiness." In the interest of being fair to the Madhyamaka system, however, it must be pointed out that the philosophy of Madhyamaka is so adamant in not taking any position in regard to "the way things really are", that even the position that "things" and sensations partake of the nature of anatman, or "no-self", is not beyond critique. Yet there is a sense in which in the traditional parlance of Buddhist thought, it may be acceptable in a general way to regard the term anatman or "no-self" as referring to the same truth of "things" and sensations as being "shunya" or "empty". What they are "empty of" is the status of being inherently or "truly-existing." We might say that although in perceptual situations we are faced with some kind of an epistemological-object or an apparent object of knowledge or perception, "its" status as an ontological-object, or as a "truly existing object" is that it is "empty" of an ontological status, or of the status of having the nature of being an inherently and "truly existing" object.

This is true of the objects of all our sensations, but it is the visual sensation and the "objects of sight" that we need to analyze in more detail, because although all the senses taken together and our thinking work together to enforce or create the view of a separate "self" interacting with a world of "truly-existing things", in a way it is our sense of sight which is perhaps the most important sense used in analyzing or understanding our world along with, of course, our thinking, which in Buddhist philosophy is regarded as being a separate type of consciousness.

We are confronted with all kinds of different "objects" or "things" in our world everyday. There are "objects" of all different sizes, shapes, and colors, in natural settings and in rooms which are in buildings, which are themselves a type of object; and also other beings such as animals and other human beings, which in a sense are another type of object with which we as an apparent subject of "self" can interact.

It may be possible to establish, through some kind of logic, the non-existence of a solid, permanent "self" who acts as the agent of our visual sensation. For example, we can try to posit the existence of such a "self" by referring to "the one who sees." But by further stating that "the one who sees, sees", it would be like establishing an agent with a double action, as we have already "accounted for" the act of seeing in the statement of "the one who sees". As it is not possible to have an agent with a double action, the statement of "the one who sees, sees" would not be logically coherent. But the use of some kind of logic may not be very helpful in trying to understand directly the non-existence of a "self" who acts as an agent in regard to the visual sensation (as well as the other sensations), so it is necessary to develop a more experiential understanding of what may actually be involved.

In regard to the so-called subjective-pole, or the "self" dimension in visual sensation, we might say that there is a deep-seated tendency to believe that there is "someone inside us" looking out onto the world of "things" and appearances from a stable vantage point "in our heads" and "behind our eyeballs". We believe that there is an ongoing-individual or "self" who "looks out" from this stable vantage point, such that there is a concrete and solid subject who looks out at all the various appearances or "things" or "objects" in our world. But this is regarded in Buddhist philosophy to be an erroneous presupposition, or a deluded view.

Through developing insight into what may actually be involved, we may find that this notion of "someone on the inside looking out" is in fact a mistaken belief, based upon the belief in a "truly existing self" and that in fact the visual sensation has nothing to do with a dimension of a "self" or even consciousness or mind "going out" to interact with or "grasp" an object of perception.

As for the objective pole of these "things" or "objects", although there appear to be very many types of "things" or "objects", there is a sense in which all of these "objects" are alike in being a mere appearance before us. Wherever we are, there is always some type of appearance before us, and people and the appearances before them always "arise together" in an inseparable manner.

In common sense thinking, we regard the appearances before us as being truly-existing "things". That is, that they are things which really "exist" in a "really-out-there" kind of way. We regard them as solid "things" that are so real that we think that "they would look like that even if we were not looking at them." We regard the world as being like some sort of container for a collection of spread-out "things" that we can interact with "here and there" and that these things are "solid things" "out there" from which we are separated by space, and that these "things" have insides which are also "solid" and "real".

The Madhyamaka philosophy is a very unusual system of philosophy, in that, rather than taking any position in regard to what is actually the case with this world of "things", it takes the approach of refuting other positions that might be taken in analyzing "the world".

Still, it may be possible to "hint at" what may be involved in an accurate analysis of the nature of appearances, the so-called "world of things". As we have said, people (and other beings, of course) and the appearances before them, always "arise together" inseparably. The key to understanding the true nature of these appearances seems to be to be aware of the dimension in which the so-called form or appearance before us and the awareness of this form or appearance, are completely inseparable. It is as if the awareness or consciousness and the form-aspect are "completely inseparable at every point" and as if the consciousness and form aspects are completely and totally integrated to create an apparitional-like appearance. Although we might say that ultimately there is no interaction between a subjective pole of consciousness, or mind, and an objective pole of separately existing form, it may still be useful to point-to the way that "things" might really be, using terms like "awareness" and "form" being "completely integrated" "beyond duality."

Also, we might say that the "mind" or "consciousness" does not "go out" to a so-called "object" but that it is as if the appearance before us has a "built in" dimension of awareness. It is not that the so called "appearance before us" is doing the "knowing" rather than the person. But we might say that appearance bears a "knowing dimension" beyond the realm of a subject sensing an object. All appearances are, in fact, non-dual (advaya). That is, they are present in the manner of an apparition, having nothing to do with any kind of truly-existing (as a separate dimension) subjective pole or "self" or "consciousness" interacting with an "actually-out-there" objective pole or "truly-existing thing."

When we say things are "apparitional" in nature, we mean that it is as if these "appearances before us" are ultimately present as if they were like a reflection in a mirror, rather than being present in a concrete, "really-out-there" kind of way. What we call "things" are really more like "apparitional-like appearances" which are present beyond the realm of a subject interacting with an independent, "truly-existing object" and which are more specifically, actually like a "surface-like apparition". By "surface-like apparition" we mean that there is a sense in which all appearances are always on the surface, as if there is a sense in which they "have nothing inside them".

Consider, for example, a common object like a box of cereal. We are presented with what we might call "a patch of color form", a mere appearance arising within the realm of our awareness. This form is completely integrated with our awareness of "it", and is ultimately present as if it were like a reflection in a mirror.

Another dimension involves a sense in which we assume that the box is a solid object with an inside that has true objective existence. But we need to develop an understanding in which "all you see is all there is" in a completely integrated situation of "completeness". Of course, we can "reveal" further dimensions of this appearance by the act called "opening the box and pouring out the contents", but it is important to keep in mind that this will actually be a further or separate non-dual visual presentation "complete" in itself, and arising beyond a subjective pole and an object interacting, which we can connect in our mind to the appearance we call "the outside of the box." But it is very important to recognize that this principle of "connecting" visual presentations over time (which also partakes ultimately of the nature of being "empty" of inherent or true existence) is only applicable at the level of conventional common sense, and that the dimension of non-dual visual presentations arising in a manner of "completeness" is the ultimate manner in which appearances arise.

Likewise, we might assume that when looking at "the front of the box" that there is a "behind" or "underneath" part of the box that is presently not visible, but which actually "exists" and "looks the way it does." But, as it is with "the inside of the box", so it is with the "behind" or the "underneath" part. We can, as with the "inside", reveal the "behind" or presently "hidden" part of the box, but the ultimate nature of the so-called "box" is the surface-like apparitional-like presentation, which is present in the manner of reflection in a mirror —a non-dual appearance beyond the realm of being a "truly-existing thing."

Let us now consider an example of the situation we might call "a person going over to their car parked across the street." From the common sense point of view, we are "over here" and we see the car which is "over there". We are the subject and the car is the object that we see, and we are separated by space. At a conventional level, we think that we can get closer to "it" by "walking towards it" until we "get there" and "pull the door handle" and "get inside the car."

Ultimately, though, the appearance we call "our car" is completely inseparable from our awareness in a non-dual way, like a miraculously-appearing apparition. "We" are completely integrated with "the appearance before us" at the so-called "first sighting" and there is a sense in which we are never separated by space from the "appearance before us." And so, in the situation called "walking over to the car," there is a sense in which "we" never actually "get closer to the car", because the appearance is completely integrated with our awareness at the so-called "first sighting" and at the so-called "subsequent sightings" as we "get closer to the car."

Similarly, the concept of "open space" as separating "us" from the "appearance before us" is ultimately also an illusion arising from not being aware of the sense in which "the appearance before us" is like a non-dual apparition, completely integrated in the realm of awareness. If there is no distance between our so-called "consciousness" and the so-called "object", there is no such thing as "invisible space" separating "us" and "the car". Also, in light of the appearance we call "our parked car" being completely integrated with non-dual awareness (keeping in mind all the different dimensions involved in the manner that has been discussed), there is a sense in which the car is not a solidly existing "thing" with an "inside" and "outside" belonging to an "it" that can be said to "truly exist" as a "thing with an inside and outside of its own."

There is also a sense in which by not recognizing the dimension of the non-dual awareness, known as vidya in Sanskrit Buddhist terminology, which is aware of the "empty" "no-self" nature of "ourselves" and "things", that by thinking that "we" and "our car" are separately existing "things" or "objects" (the word "object" can be broken down etymologically to mean "thrown-against"), we actually create or enforce the illusion that we are a separate, truly existing "thing" bounded by skin, walking around and regarding the world as a collection of "things" with which to interact. By believing that we are "walking over to our car and getting inside this thing", it is as if we solidify or actually create the belief that we are a truly existing "thing" which exists as "just another thing" which is separated from the appearances before us.

Ultimately the scientific notion of people (and other beings with consciousness, such as animals) as being organisms which interact with an environment which is separate from them, is an erroneous view, according to Buddhist philosophy. It is true that, in a sense, as people we are an "embodiment of mind". But this mind is a completely open-ended continuum which is so open-ended that, in a sense, it is as if the mind has the ability to "take on the form" of "whatever happens to appear before it", that is, the appearances which we regard as being "truly existing things." Although from the ultimate point of view, this "mind" is as "empty" of true or inherent existence as is the "self" or "things", it may still be useful to talk about our being an "embodiment of mind" which becomes terminated by appearances in a non-dual way. beyond the realm of a subject interacting with an object, in order to "point to" the way things may be ultimately.

Also, the idea of the environment of "the world of things", as being a realm separate from the "beings in the world", as if "the world of things" were "standing around" separately, "waiting to be interacted with", needs to be analyzed more carefully.

Consider, for example, the idea of famous landmarks, such as the White House and the Kremlin. We might say that these are, in conventional thinking, regarded as actually "taking up space in a certain place" and having the status of "really being there and standing around looking like they look" and having the status of a "truly-existing thing in a truly-existing place." It may be possible to undermine this notion of "things" and "places" "waiting for us" in a separate manner. We might be able to end up with a more sophisticated understanding of how it is with these "people", "places", and "things" in a manner that goes beyond the realm of organisms interacting with a solid world of things that "stand around" as a separate environment.

From the point of view of what may actually be involved in the situation called "an American looking at the Kremlin" or "a Russian looking at the White House", if we understand this idea of ourselves as an "embodiment of mind" which becomes "terminated" by an appearance in a completely non-dual way, beyond the realm of a subject and object, it may be necessary to completely rethink our ideas of analyzing the world as being made up of separate "categories" of "people", "places" and "things", which would also have far-reaching ramifications in the sociopolitical and other realms. And if, in this light of our being an "embodiment of a mind" which becomes "terminated" by an appearance in a non-dual way beyond the realm of subject and object, we consider that, for example, in a subject such as the history of warfare or aggression, we are dealing with soldiers of different nations, as embodiments of mind, whose minds, from a higher point of view, become "terminated" in a non-dual way by the appearances referred to at a common-sense conventional level, as "other soldiers who are the enemy," the implications are shocking, in a manner that goes beyond, and yet encompasses, the realm of moral considerations. In this example, rather than labeling this manifestation of our mind to be "our enemy", the natural "expression" of our non-dual awareness would be to have compassion for these illusory beings, and to act accordingly.

As for the active aspect of this non-dual awareness which is beyond the realm of subject and object, or vidya, this is termed jnana, and as opposed to vijnana, or ordinary dualistic consciousness in which the subjective and objective poles are regarded as being actually inherently existing, with jnana, one is aware of the non-dual nature of people and appearances. If we use an example of "two people and their parked car", we might say that the person using vijnana regards the car as a truly existing thing that he or she can "walk over to and get inside of", while the person using jnana is aware of the non-dual dimension in which the "individual" and the "thing" are both "empty" of being actually existing things which are interacting with each other.

From the point of view of the person whose awareness is characterized as vijnana (which can be broken down etymologically to mean "knowing-apart"), there are three separate things involved in this example: that is, two people plus one car. From the point of view of the person whose awareness would be characterized as jnana, however, this is not actually the case. But what "actually is the case" may be beyond the realm of being expressed in the ordinary language of "people and things" as separate objects to be "added up" and of "two people interacting with one same thing." Of course, the person using jnana is still aware of the sense in which things like cereal boxes and cars appear to exist at a conventional level, that is, the way the seem to exist from the point of view of "other people using vijnana"; but he/she is never separated from the non-dual awareness of vidya, and this is what is said to characterize the awareness of the Buddhas.

If we mistake the appearances before us as being "truly existing", "actually-out-there" types of "things" with true, inherent existence, we fall into deep error, according to Buddhist thought, setting up a fictitious realm of an individual separated from the world of appearances (so-called "things") in a deep-seated way. This is known as the realm of samsara, the world of "running around and around in circles", chasing after "things" we regard as "really existing" that we would like to have, while avoiding "the things that we don't like." But these emotions of attachment or desire, and aversion or anger, as well as the other basic emotions of pride and jealousy, all arise from dualistic-ignorance or "not knowing how it really is with people and things". It is said that this realm of samsara and its "flip-side" of nirvana, exist nowhere else than in our mind: when our mind is pervaded by emotional and intellectual obscurations about "the way things are", we are caught up in samsara; but when this same mind is completely freed from these obscurations, we attain nirvana. So nirvana is not some other-worldly realm in which we would see different things than other people see, but our same world seen differently; that is, pervaded by the non-dual awareness of vidya.

Also, our mind in union with the ultimate "empty" nature of appearances is actually the Dharmakaya, the so-called "Body of Truth" of a Buddha, which is one of the "three bodies of a Buddha". In addition, while the relative-Bodhichitta, the so-called "mind of enlightenment" may be considered to be compassion, as well as the aspiration to attain perfect enlightenment for the benefit of all beings (along with doing whatever we can to help other beings), the ultimate-Bodhichitta consists of the wisdom of the awareness of "emptiness". So it is considered essential to conjoin compassion with wisdom in order to attain perfect enlightenment, the level of a Buddha.

Although we begin with the common sense view of "people" and "things" as truly-existing separate entities interacting with each other, after we hear about, reflect upon, and meditate on the "empty" or no-self nature of people and things, (while also having accumulated a vast store of "merit" or "positive energy", through virtuous actions of our body, speech and mind), we may begin to engage in the process of "the turning over in the mind" by which we begin to "tune-into" the ultimate, "empty" nature of "people" and "appearances". Little by little, we can deepen our awareness of this dimension until it becomes more and more a part of our nature, and eventually, it may be possible to become a true embodiment of this non-dual awareness, or vidya.

When the Buddhist texts were first being translated in Tibet, the term vidya, or non-dual awareness, was translated into Tibetan as rig-pa. But, rather than translating the negation of this non-dual awareness of vidya (avidya) as rig-med, which would indicate a complete negation of rig-pa, it was translated as ma-rig-pa, indicating a qualitative drop in the level of rig-pa, or non-dual awareness. So we can see that from one point of view, our awareness of the nature of "people" and "things" is not completely confused, but that it needs to be transformed so that it will be "in tune-with" "the way things really are".

Although in Hinduism, the different yogas are practiced in order to attain union with God, in Buddhism, we might say that "emptiness-yoga", that is, trying to attain union with the ultimate, "empty" (apparitional) nature of people and appearances, is practiced. The teachings on the "empty" (apparitional) nature of "people" and appearances (so-called "things") are a fundamental teaching of Mahayana Buddhism, which are also very important in the offshoot of the Mahayana, known as Vajrayana or Tantric Buddhism. But even though the teachings on the "empty" or no-self nature of "people" and "things" are a fundamental teaching of the Mahayana, at the highest level of Vajrayana Buddhism, known as Dzogchen, or the "Great Perfection", it is in fact the continual contemplation of the non-dual awareness of vidya (rig-pa)which is said to constitute the main practice of this highest mystical system of Dzogchen.

In this highest Buddhist mystical system of Dzogchen, the practitioner is directly introduced to the non-dual awareness (vidya or rig-pa) by their teacher, and takes the continual contemplation of the true Nature of Mind (and reality) as their central practice. Recognizing that all thoughts are, in fact, "empty" of belonging to a "self", all thoughts are continually "self-liberated", arising from and dissolving back into the continuum of the Dharmakaya, like waves arising and dissolving back into the ocean. At the same time, the practitioner continually contemplates the inseparable union of appearance and "emptiness."

It is regarded as being very important to cultivate the awareness of the non-dual nature of "people" and "things" in regard to all manner of appearances, deepening our understanding of what this means until it becomes part of our being at a very deep and completely integrated level. When we begin trying to understand the meaning of shunyata or the "empty" (apparitional) nature of appearances, it may seem as if it is easier to recognize this dimension of apparitionalness in regard to some "things" in a more readily comprehensible way than with other "things." But we should eventually try to understand this "empty" apparitional nature of things in regard to all appearances, although we may find it useful to "practice" using objects where we find this non-dual awareness more apparent.

Along with the idea that appearances are "shunya" (or partake of the nature of shunyata or "emptiness") or "empty of inherent existence", in the manner that has been discussed, in the Vajrayana or Tantric teachings, it is said that there exists also a dimension of luminosity; that is, that we are endowed with a knowing capacity, or an ability to see "things" with complete clarity, "as they are". Also, these appearances may be characterized as partaking of the nature of "non-dividedness"; that is, that they are completely "nondivided" in regard to the subject and object, or more precisely, "non-divided" beyond the realm of a supposed subject and object.

In regard to these three dimensions, it is said that "emptiness" manifests as the Dharmakaya body of a Buddha; "luminosity" as the Sambhogakaya; and that the inseparable union of "emptiness" and "luminosity" manifests as the Nirmanakaya.

As a footnote to these three dimensions of appearance, we might consider the myth of Lucifer in the Judeo-Christian tradition. Lucifer means the "light-bearer" and if we examine this myth from the proper angle, we might find that this myth of the fall of Lucifer may actually refer to the "fall of man" from being in union with the ultimate, "empty", luminous dimension of non-dual awareness, into the realm of individuals regarding these appearances as being truly-existing in a "real", "out-there" kind of way.

In Mahayana and Vajrayana Buddhism, although the term tathagatagarbha can be taken in general usage to refer to the enlightened Buddha-nature inherent in all beings, existing as a potentiality that needs to be activated and actualized, in another sense it refers to the process by which Being itself is led back to attaining its true state. Since this level of attainment is beyond the level of a "self" who has attained this level of realization, there is a sense in which the realization or attainment belongs to Being itself, rather than to a "self" or "I".

Then it may be possible to understand such notions as that what is behind the nature of "people" and "appearances" is nothing more than the playful nature (lila) of Being itself. It seems that Being has the ability to "set-up" apparitional-like appearances, but it must be understood that these appearances are completely "empty" of true or inherent existence, in the manner that has been discussed. The nature of these appearances is the completely miraculous display or manifestation of Being, by which it "mirrors" or "looks at" itself, but in regard to their status of being truly-existing "things", they are alike in never having come into actual existence, ultimately. As the renowned Tibetan poet-lama Milarepa expressed it: "Things appear, but they don't really exist!"

If-we were to attain this level of being a true embodiment or a "holder" of the non-dual awareness, or a vidyadhara, developing this awareness to ever-increasing levels until we embody this awareness at a level of total realization, while at the same time being able to act in a completely skillful and compassionate manner in regard to these apparitional-like appearances of "beings" and "things", it is said that there is nothing further to attain or realize; nothing higher to which we would need to aspire.

As the renowned Tibetan lama of the Dzogchen tradition of Tibetan Buddhism, Longchen Rabjampa, has said: "Since everything is but an apparition, perfect in being what it is, having nothing to do with good or bad, acceptance or rejection, one may well burst out in laughter!"

The Primordial Buddha, Samantabhadra, with consort, Samantabhadri

The Last Word In Shalom Is Om

Namgyalma, The Victorious aspect of the mind of the Buddha,
and the Goddess of Long Life

As we begin the new millennium, the world's population now totals over six billion human beings. Humankind is composed of many different races of people, with people of many ethnic and religious backgrounds, living in many separate countries around the globe.

According to Buddhist ways of reckoning time, we are currently living in the "degenerate age" of the Kali Yuga, a period in world history when we are all especially subject to the negative emotions, such as anger, hatred, and attachment, all of which are said to arise from the fundamental condition of ignorance: that is, ignorance of the true nature of the individual, and the nature of the world of phenomena around us.

If we first look at the nature of the individual, on the surface it may seem that we are all very different. Because of these differences in race, religion, and nationality, etc., our collective human consciousness is endowed with a strong sense of separateness from one individual to another, and from one ethnic or national group to another. One is reminded of the late psychiatrist, R.D. Laing's rendering of the word "individual" as "in-divide-you-all." Because of this feeling of lack of unity among all people, we remain as a world of many separate individuals and groups, and are unaware of the common thread that underlies the fabric composing the tapestry of humanity. This lack of awareness may be said to be the source of the underlying tension and difficulty which prevent us from living together in a world of peace and harmony.

Along with meaning both "hello" and "goodbye," the Hebrew word for "peace" is "shalom." It may be interesting to note that the last two letters of shalom spell the sacred Sanskrit syllable, OM. Among the three syllables, OM AH HUM, regarded in Vajrayana Buddhism as the expression of the enlightened nature of the individual's body, speech, and mind, it is OM which is the syllable representing the aspect of "body," or embodiment. If we truly seek peace among all the people of the world, we may need to look more carefully at the nature of human embodiment, in order to find what it is that we all have in common; what it is that makes us all not different, but essentially all the same.

As human beings, we have a body composed of flesh, blood, muscle, tissue, and bones; internal organs, such as the stomach, heart, and lungs; sense organs, such as the eyes, ears, and nose, and so forth.

Although we may all look different facially, and with a variety of body-types, the components of our bodies are essentially the same. The insides of our bodies are "put together" in basically the same way, and are comprised of building blocks of cells, which are essentially the same from one individual to another. And at the genetic level, minor differences notwithstanding, our makeup varies very little from one individual to another. Even at the level of the invisible "energy body" composed of energy channels (called tsa in Tibetan Buddhist terminology), energy currents (called lung), and concentrated energy drops (called tigle), we are all essentially "built the same."

In conventional, common sense thinking, we regard this body as "our home;" that is, as the place in which the individual or self—the person we refer to as "I," resides. We say or think, "This is my body. I have a head, chest, back, arms, legs, hands, and feet," and so forth. But suppose we were to "venture mentally" inside our body to see where this "self" is located? We would see the internal tissue, bones, and blood, and the organs such as the stomach, brain, heart, and lungs. But looking carefully and with an open mind, we may find that it is not possible to consider any of these components as being our "self" or "I." Although we usually assume that there is "someone inside us who lives in our body," or that we are "the sum total of all our parts," if we look carefully, mentally dissecting the inside of the body down to the level of cells, and even further to the level of molecules, atoms, and sub-atomic particles, in no location will we ever ultimately find this self or "I"; that is, the person we refer to by our name. So in a sense, we are composed internally of all this "stuff," but ultimately, there is also a sense in which all people are basically alike in the condition of having "no-self" who inhabits or "lives in" the body.

It may be argued by some that, although the self or "I" cannot ultimately be found somewhere in the body, that the self is "the one who inhabits our mind," and "does our thinking." We may think, "My name is such-and-such, and I am this being who lives in my body and has consciousness. I look out at the outside world of things, and think different thoughts about the world I see around me."

However, if we look into the nature of "the one who thinks," and the nature of the thoughts that arise in our mind, we may need to reevaluate our original assumptions about "the self who lives in our mind." The mind is endowed with the energy and capacity to produce thoughts. If we use the analogy of the mind being like a body of water, such as a lake, the thoughts that arise can be likened to waves arising on the surface of the lake. However, we go astray when we assume that there is "someone in our mind who is having these thoughts."

Consider, for example, the nature of a thought that might arise, such as, "My name is Charlie, and I am sitting here thinking "We need to recognize that what is ultimately involved is a case of "a thought claiming to be a 'somebody (or "I") having a thought'!" This thought actually arises as the creative play of our awareness, but we wrongly assume that the thought has "an individual behind it;" that is, the supposed "I" who is "creating or thinking the thoughts."

To refer back to the previous analogy, we can begin to recognize the so-called "thoughts in our mind" as arising like waves on the surface of the lake of our mind, while seeing through the facade of there being a concrete individual or self who is "saying and hearing the thoughts." We can practice the "cutting through" (called trekcho in Tibetan) the solidity of the ego, remaining in and cultivating the non-dual awareness, and relaxing in an undistracted way in "the natural state." In this state, we allow thoughts to arise from and dissolve back into "the lake of our mind," all the while recognizing the thoughts and emotions as being the natural expression of our mind, but being aware that there is ultimately no self or person, or "I" who inhabits our body and mind. In this way, thoughts and emotions arise from and dissolve back into the mind, like waves on water, and are continually "freed" in a process of "self-liberation."

So in a sense, all people are alike in having a body and mind, but ultimately being endowed with the nature of having "no-self" who inhabits the body and mind. Although on a conventional level, it may be true for a person to claim that "I'm a Caucasian," or "I'm a Christian," or "I'm a Russian," at a deeper level of truth, this "I" is found to be "empty of inherent existence," as an individual who "lives in the body and mind, and has an identity."

. But this "selfless" or "empty" nature is not a total void, like a mere blankness. Although there may be no concrete individual or "I" inhabiting the body/mind complex, as an embodiment of a mind, we are still endowed with a knowing capacity, or cognizance, and we can still know and see things with a sense of clarity. Although thoughts arise without "ownership," they still arise as the natural display of our cognizing awareness.

So we might say that all beings are alike in having the same nature of mind: this nature of mind is "empty" of being endowed with a concrete individual, or "I," yet is at the same time, cognizant, knowing, and aware. These two aspects are said to be completely inseparable, such that we can refer to the nature of mind as being characterized by the inseparable union of "emptiness" (called tongpa-nyid in Tibetan) and clarity (or luminosity—called od-sal in Tibetan). The unity of these two aspects expresses itself as compassion, that is, as compassion for all other beings who have not recognized their true nature. In another sense, this inseparable unity of "emptiness" and "clarity" (called saltong-yermed in Tibetan), manifests as the capacity for wisdom, compassion, and the ability to help others.

To summarize, the essence (nowo in Tibetan) of the nature of mind is "empty" of an individual or "I" who inhabits the mind; yet the mind's nature (rangzhin in Tibetan) is that it is cognizant and knowing; and the "energy" of the unity of these two inseparable aspects is endowed with the "capacity" (tugje in Tibetan) for knowledge, kindness, and the ability to benefit others. These three aspects (essence, nature, and capacity) taken together as an inseparable unity represent the true nature of mind (called sem-nyid in Tibetan), and are also referred to as the "Buddha-nature."

But what of the nature of the world of appearances that surrounds us? At a conventional level, we are surrounded by furniture, and objects in rooms which are in buildings, located in an environment of towns and cities, and existing within natural settings we regard as "the environment" or "the outside world."

In Mahayana Buddhist philosophy, this world of objects and appearances also partakes of the "empty" or "no-self" nature. In a similar way to thoughts and emotions arising as the "display of our non-dual awareness" (rigpai-tsal in Tibetan), all appearances (called nangwa in Tibetan), including the objects of the other senses, such as hearing, also arise as the creative display of our own awareness.

We might say that our mind is like a "magic mirror" which reflects the world of appearances around it. These appearances are alike in being a mere reflection in the mirror of our mind. Appearances are said to be like an apparition, in the sense that they have no inherent existence apart from our mind's perception, and are like a "surface-like reflection" appearing in the "magic mirror of mind"—appearing, and yet not truly existing "from their own side." The aspect of things being not-truly existent is the "empty" aspect (called tongpa in Tibetan); while the sense in which things still appear is the aspect of clarity (salwa in Tibetan).

So there is a sense in which we "project" the world of appearances around us, with all so-called objects being a manifestation of the nature of mind or of "mind-itself." A useful analogy to indicate this condition is that of the turtle, who carries his shell as a home everywhere he goes. Similarly, we are said to be like "a Buddha in a Buddha-field," who recognizes his environment of "the world of things," as not something outside of and separate from himself, but as the "ornament" of his awareness; that is, as a manifestation and aspect of his own non-dual awareness. This intrinsic awareness, or non-dual awareness, is known as rigpa in the Dzogchen system of teachings of Tibetan Buddhism.

For example, suppose two people are "looking at a building." The person caught up in dualistic thinking characterized by ignorance, along with regarding himself as a "truly-existing self," regards the building as being located "over there at a distance," and as being truly-existing independent of his perception. That is, his body is considered to be like a "thing" that walks around and perceives and has thoughts about things that seem to exist "from their own side," such as buildings.

For the individual aware of the non-dual dimension, however, buildings and other phenomena are regarded as not being separate from his awareness. These appearances are instead recognized as a direct manifestation of one's own mind, or non-dual awareness, and this recognition may be said to be ineffable and beyond characterization, yet still understandable within the realm of our knowledge. So the person whose mind is inseparable from intrinsic awareness can still deal appropriately with conventionally existing objects, such as "a cup of tea on the table in a room in a building," yet always remains inseparable from the awareness of things as an apparition or reflection existing within the realm of the mind.

Going back to the image of the turtle and his shell, it is of vital importance that we recognize the sense in which we "project" the world of phemenona around us everywhere we go; that we are, in fact, "a Buddha in a Buddha-field." In the system of todgal ("crossing over") in the Dzogchen teachings, it is said that what we perceive as "the outside world" is actually "the clear light of the mind," which is projected from within the heart center through the invisible channels that run from the heart to the eyes, and that what we perceive as "the outside world" is actually our own "clear light awareness."

By way of conclusion, consider, for example, a situation that might be characterized as "someone looking at people in a building in a foreign country." If we overlook the dimension of non-duality, or the sense in which all appearances are like a reflection in the mirror of our mind, arising beyond the level of subject and object, we solidify a fluid and open-ended world into a world of solid objects divided by imaginary boundaries, which can only lead to conflict, through not being "in-sync" with the fundamental nature of reality.

On the one hand, we seem to be "standing alone" or separately, as an individual, separate from truly-existing "things in different places;" and think that these buildings and cities and countries, as well as the inhabitants in the buildings and cities, etc. "stand around" in a manner completely independent of our awareness. This lack of awareness of the true nature of subject and object then gives rise to the various negative emotions. By solidifying the sense of the objects of our attachment as being truly-existing, we also solidify our illusory ego-nature; and we also experience negative emotions, such as anger and fear of what we regard as being separate and different from ourselves. This process "snowballs" or spins out of control, until we end up with the current situation of billions of individuals existing in a relatively small space, yet having very little sense of unity, and with not much "peace on earth" or even peace of mind!

Yet through study, reflection, and meditation on the Buddha-nature; that is, the true nature of mind (sem-nyid)—which is also the true nature of reality (cho-nyid)—we can realize our potential for enlightenment, purifying our body/mind of negative qualities, and developing or perfecting our positive qualities; and our awareness of our true nature. Recognizing all beings and all appearances everywhere as one all-inclusive "mandala," or configuration of unity and wholeness, the space of the Earth will inherently be endowed with peace and harmony among all beings. Rather than focusing on the sense in which we are all different, we will all recognize that all people (and for that matter, all beings) possess the Buddha-nature, and the same true nature of mind, and of reality.

So in this regard, considering the sacred syllable, OM, as an expression of the principle of enlightened embodiment, it is through investigating, cultivating, and realizing the true nature of our embodiment as human beings, that peace on earth will come, as we keep in mind that "the last word in shalom is OM." In this way, peace and understanding and harmony among all humanity will arise as we develop our knowledge and understanding of the true nature of our existence, and as our actions become inseparable from our knowledge.

Recommended Reading

The Words of My Perfect Teacher, Patrul Rinpoche (translated Padmakara Translation Group), San Francisco: Harper Collins, 1994.

The Three Levels of Spiritual Perception, Deshung Rinpoche (translated Jared Rhoton), Boston: Wisdom, 1995.

A Guide to the Bodhisattva's Way of Life, Shantideva (translated Stephen Batchelor), Dharamsala: Library of Tibetan Works and Archives, 1979.

Bodhicitta—Cultivating the Compassionate Mind of Enlightenment, Ven. Lobsang Gyatso (translated Ven. Sherab Gyatso), Ithaca: Snow Lion, 1997.

Compassion—The Key to Great Awakening, Geshe Tsultim Gyeltsen, Boston: Wisdom, 1997.

Advice From a Spiritual Friend, Geshe Rabten and Geshe Dhargyey (translated Brian Beresford), Boston: Widsom, 1977.

Ceaseless Echoes of the Great Silence, Khenpo Palden Sherab (translated Khenpo Tsewang Dongyal), Boca Raton, FL :Sky Dancer Press, 1993.

The Gelug-Kagyu Tradition of Mahamudra, H.H. The Dalai Lama and Alexander Berzin, Ithaca: Snow Lion, 1997.

Songs of Naropa, Thrangu Rinpoche (translated Erik Pema Kunsang), Kathmandu: Rangjung Yeshe, 1997.

Rainbow Painting, Tulku Urgyen Rinpoche (translated Erik Pema Kunsang), Kathmandu: Rangjung Yeshe, 1995.

Indisputable Truth, Chokyi Nyima Rinpoche (translated Erik Pema Kunsang), Kathmandu: Rangjung Yeshe, 1996.

You Are the Eyes of the World, Longchenpa (translated Kennard Lipman and Merrill Peterson), Novato, CA: Lotsawa, 1987.

The Four-Themed Precious Garland, Longchenpa (translated Alexander Berzin), Dharamsala: Library of Tibetan Works and Archives, 1978.

The Cycle of Day and Night Namkhai Norbu (translated John Reynolds), Barrytown, NY: Station Hill Press, 1984.

Buddhahood Without Meditation, Dudjom Lingpa (translated Richard Barron), Junction City, CA: Padma Publishing, 1994.

Introduction to the Nature of the Mind, Yangthang Rinpoche (translated Sangye Khandro), Mt. Shasta, CA: Yeshe Melong,1994.

The Union of Dzogchen and Mahamudra, Yangthang Rinpoche (translated Sangye Khandro), Mt. Shasta, CA: Yeshe Melong,1996.

A quote from The Perfect Dynamic Energy of the Lion: “Throughout the three times (i.e. past. present, and future), Buddahood is awareness free of dualistic perception.”

The dharmapala (protectress), Ekajati

THIS IS THE END OF THE BOOK—